SHE

Kathryn Tucker Windham

1918–2011

Also by Kathryn Tucker Windham

Treasured Alabama Recipes (1967)

13 Alabama Ghosts and Jeffrey (1969)

Jeffrey Introduces 13 More Southern Ghosts (1971)

Treasured Tennessee Recipes (1972)

Treasured Georgia Recipes (1973)

13 Georgia Ghosts and Jeffrey (1973)

13 Mississippi Ghosts and Jeffrey (1974)

Exploring Alabama (1974)

Alabama: One Big Front Porch (1975)

13 Tennessee Ghosts and Jeffrey (1977)

The Ghost in the Sloss Furnaces (1978)

Southern Cooking to Remember (1978)

Count Those Buzzards! Stamp Those Grey Mules! (1979)

Jeffrey's Latest 13: More Alabama Ghosts (1982)

A Serigamy of Stories (1983)

Odd–Egg Editor (1990)

The Autobiography of a Bell (1991)

A Sampling of Selma Stories (1991)

My Name is Julia (1991)

Twice Blessed (1996)

Encounters (1998)

The Bridal Wreath Bush (1999)

Common Threads (2000)

It's Christmas! (2002)

Ernest's Gift (2004)

Jeffrey's Favorite 13 Ghost Stories (2004)

Alabama, One Big Front Porch (2007)

Spit, Scarey Ann and Sweat Bees (2009)

She

The Old Woman Who
Took Over My Life

~

KATHRYN TUCKER
WINDHAM

NEWSOUTH BOOKS
Montgomery

NewSouth Books
105 S. Court Street
Montgomery, AL 36104

Library of Congress Cataloging-in-Publication Data

Windham, Kathryn Tucker.
She : the old woman who took over my life /
Kathryn Tucker Windham.
p. cm.

ISBN: 978-1-58838-278-8 (pbk.)
ISBN: 978-1-60306-103-2 (ebk.)

1. Windham, Kathryn Tucker. 2. Folklorists—Alabama—
Biography. 3. Journalists—Alabama—Biography. 4. Alabama—
Social life and customs. I. Title.
CT275.W584525A3 2011+
976.1092—dc23
[B]

2011038310

Design by Randall Williams

Printed in the United States of America by Maple Press

To Ben and Dilcy,

who helped me put

She in her place.

Contents

She MOVES IN

I can't recall when I became aware that an old woman was nudging her way into my life. At first her presence was hardly noticeable, but as my years soared into the nineties, it was no longer possible to ignore her presence. She disrupts my plans, demands my attention, shames me into completing abandoned projects, requires nutritious meals, curtails my away-from-home activities, hides things from me, makes my handwriting less legible, and pushes names and events into the deepest crevices of my mind even while prodding me to tell and write old family stories and traditions.

Sometimes acquaintances, many two or three decades younger than I am, ask, "Now that you have curtailed your travels, what do you do with all your spare time?"

I laugh. "Spare time? I don't have any. I am the

caregiver for a crotchety old woman and that's a full-time assignment." Then I have to explain that I am not a nurse, I do not get paid, and although I have known the woman for as long as I can remember, I am still surprised by my role as her primary caregiver.

It is not a job I applied for.

Since I'm not a nurse, it is fortunate that my charge does not need nursing care. She does need to be reminded to take her medicine and to use her eye drops.

I REFER TO my ward as "*She*." Most of the time *She* and I get along rather well, but *She*—in her old age— seems to have become more opinionated, more set in her ways, more interested in what happened years ago than in today's news. *She* used to read three newspapers every day and read a national news magazine weekly. Now *She* barely scans our thin local paper, and stacks of unread copies of *Time* gather under the edge of her bed. When I mention the growing accumulation of reading material, *She* promises to "have a big throwing-away. Soon! Very soon!"

Though her reading is curtailed, *She* continues to write a little—on a rather strange assortment of topics. A casual remark can set her off. Recently, a guest mentioned General McArthur, and *She* immediately recalled his statement, "Old soldiers never die, they just fade away."

"He could have done better than that," *She* commented, and for several days afterwards, *She* showed me variations she had written on the general theme of departing this life . . . lines such as "old explorers never die, they just get lost," and "old quarterbacks never die, they just pass away."

My amusement egged her on, and *She* wrote more. There was "old radio announcers never die, they just sign off." And "old runners never die, they just cross the finish line"; "old jockeys never die, they just drop the reins"; "old readers never die, they just turn the final page." When I stopped laughing at her efforts, *She* stopped showing them to me. There are likely dozens more under her bed with the untouched issues of *Time*.

I wonder if *She* has written one for herself, or for me. Probably not, because *She* has been too busy nagging me about neglected, half-finished projects I should have attended to long ago.

"YOU NEED TO clean off your desk," *She* told me recently. "How long has it been since you've seen the top? Get rid of that clutter!"

My desk sits beneath the window of my bedroom/office, the largest room in my house. The desktop is solid oak, five and a half feet long and two feet wide. It is supported by curved wrought iron legs with the face of a Roman god on each foot. The worn surface is ideal for writing (I use yellow legal pads) and for "putting things on." There is even a long, wide filigreed iron shelf between the legs to hold spillover clutter.

That desk came out of my father's office at the bank in Thomasville, Alabama. I have three other things from his bank.

First is one of the bank's checks, with my eldest sister Edith's picture on it. Daddy had two sons, but when a beautiful baby daughter came along he was so proud that he had her picture printed on all the bank's checks. That was a long time ago, 1901 or 1902, I believe.

Then I have a paperweight with a stone base on which three monkeys sit in the familiar pose: one has his hands over his ears, one has his hands over his eyes, and the last has his hands over his mouth. Their words of wisdom are carved around the base: "Hear No Evil, Speak No Evil, See No Evil." The number 235 is carved on the back, so I suppose this was a limited edition of a popular paperweight. Chipped and discolored by decades of use and age, it is easily the ugliest item in my house but I treasure it because it reminds me of Daddy's philosophy.

My third small "relic" is a needle case. Printed on the front are the words:

COMPLIMENTS OF FARMER'S BANK AND TRUST CO.
THOMASVILLE, ALA.
CAPITAL $100,000.00
UNDIVIDED PROFITS $25,000.00
"PIONEERS OF WEST ALABAMA."

Inside are an assortment of needles, small calendars for 1910 and 1911, an advertisement for the bank showing a well-dressed man pulling an equally well-dressed but dripping wet woman out of the water. "*We can help you out*," the caption says. On the back is an explanation of the gift, saying, in effect, that the needles "point the way to the bank."

I wish I still had one of the metal baseball-shaped banks that once were given to Thomasville children to encourage them to open their own savings accounts.

Most of what money came my way went into one of those little cast-iron banks. I never had an allowance. Mother told me years later that when I was offered an allowance, my feelings were hurt by the idea of being paid each week like a servant. I preferred to look under the brass candlestick on the mantel in my parents' bedroom where they put loose change for general use.

I did fill my baseball bank often enough to make several deposits into my father's bank. When the bank failed in the early 1930s, I was wiped out financially, lost my life savings. But that was the least of it.

I learned of the bank failure while I was in Mobile on a school trip. The Thomasville High School band used to go to Mobile to march and play in the Mardi Gras parades. We rode in a flatbed truck which had sides and benches added to its bed. Riding it a hundred miles to Mobile took a long while and was not comfortable.

I rode in my first streetcar in Mobile. At one point I pulled the cord by my seat, the car stopped, and the conductor helped me off. I was too embarrassed to tell him I had not known what the cord was for and had not reached my destination, so, tired though I was, I had to walk about another half mile.

When I got home the next day, my father asked, "Did you bring any money home from Mobile?"

"Yes, sir. I brought three or four dollars."

"Then that is all the money we have in the world," he told me.

THUS I WAS introduced to the Great Depression. We

survived. People who owed money to my father paid in produce or whatever they had. I recall buckets of yellow and green label Alaga syrup lined around the whole baseboards in our kitchen.

After Daddy died in the summer of 1936, we lost our house and all of our furniture except for the glass-front bookcases with their hundreds of books, most of which I still own.

I also have a small cherry drop-leaf table that was by my father's bed. Its drawer still smells of his Prince Albert tobacco and his pipe.

Mother and I moved in with Aunt Bet and Tabb—who was Mother's age—in their house behind ours, facing the highway to Grove Hill.

The piece of furniture I miss most is our dining room table. Aunt Bet brought it from Texas to Thomasville when she came home to live. Actually, she came home to have her second baby, a little girl bearing the family name Tabb. Arrangements for the trip back to Thomasville had been made when her four-year-old son Jamie broke out with measles. Aunt Bet was never a woman to be deterred. She put a hat and veil on Jamie to hide his measles spots and came on the train, no doubt spreading measles across four states on that long journey.

Aunt Bet never returned to Texas. She never mentioned her husband's name again. None of the members of the family ever knew what happened to him.

In addition to Jamie and the measles, Aunt Bet did bring home her dining room table, a massive piece of furniture. It was solid oak and could be extended with leaves to seat twenty people. The legs were hand-carved dragons, complete with scales and big mouths. As a child, I liked to play under that table, pretending to ride those dragons. After Aunt Bet's death, the table was sold.

After I was married, with Byrd Goodman's help I tracked down the new owner of the table and tried to buy it. I explained how I enjoyed riding these dragons when I was a little girl.

"My children like to ride them, too," she said, and she would not sell it.

Craftsmen in a Texas prison made that table. I

still want it. And I still wish I had kept one of those baseball banks.

SEE? *She* STARTED me on a project but I haven't thrown away a single piece of paper on my desk, have not even arranged any neat stacks of stuff. *She* makes me waste so much time!

All *She* managed to do was remind me of a favorite piece of doggerel:

Cleaning Up

No matter how
I shred and toss
This aging clutter
Still is boss.

I expedite
With all my might,
But still this room
Is a messy sight!

Cooking for *She*

Friends are thoughtful about bringing food: jellies, preserves, pies, cakes, homemade rolls and biscuits, Brunswick stew, figs, peaches, country syrup, and vegetables fresh from the garden (I like to shuck the corn, pull off all the silks, and eat it raw, right off the cob). But ninety-two-year-old appetites can't deal with the bounty—every bit of it appreciated. Some days I am tempted to open a curb market on my sidewalk!

I'm a right good cook (simple foods) so meals are no major problem. *She* and I do argue occasionally about the prolonged use of leftovers. Being a child of the Great Depression, I have a hard time throwing anything away, especially food.

My mother and Aunt Bet were brag cooks. Their reputations for making cakes, candies, date logs, chicken salad and rolls were unchallenged in the

Thomasville community. I can close my eyes now and still hear Aunt Bet saying, "Tiptoe through the kitchen. Don't shake the floor. I have a cake in the oven."

When I was a little girl our kitchen was in a building in the backyard, unattached to the house. Many Southern kitchens were.

I liked to cook until *She* arrived on the scene. Now everything takes so much longer to do. By the time I plan the menu, prepare the meal, eat and wash dishes, it's time for exercise and a nap. Medicine must be taken then, too.

Then it is time to start all over again. There is barely time for the other thing *She* and I do a lot of, remembering the past.

WHEN I WAS a child, everyone rested after a big noon meal, especially in the heat of summer afternoons. Rest time was over when I heard the windlass on our well squeaking. Somebody was drawing water for lemonade, and making lemonade was my assignment. I squeezed lemons, measured sugar, stirred it well in one of Mother's big pitchers and cooled it with chunks of ice from the dwindling block in the icebox on the screen porch.

She reminded me that Oma, the delivery man from Mrs. Wilkinson's icehouse, always filled the metal-lined chamber of our icebox when he made his Monday rounds in his horse-drawn wagon loaded with big blocks of ice. If I met him down the street, Oma would let me eat slivers of ice that broke off when he chipped a customer's smaller block of ice from the big blocks on the back of his wagon.

In the summertime, when we had iced tea and made ice cream, we needed two deliveries a week. *She* laughed about the summer when my brother Wilson was so involved with playing baseball that he neglected his duty of keeping the drip pan under the icebox emptied. The pan overflowed, the floor rotted and the icebox fell to the ground. Daddy was not amused.

BEING SO MUCH younger than my siblings, I was the family pet, but Daddy was strict with my brothers.

As a teenager, Wilson had to get Daddy's bank ready for business each day. He swept the floors, emptied the wastebaskets, sharpened the pencils, filled the inkwells, saw that there was tape in the adding machines, and filled the big jug that supplied water for the drinking fountain. All this had to be done before the bank opened at 8 A.M.

She interrupted my train of thought by reminding me Wilson always said that our older brothers, when they didn't have other chores, had to move the woodpile from one side of the backyard to the other, stacking it neatly. Daddy believed that idleness bordered on sinfulness.

I have few memories of those two older brothers, Wood and Jamie. They were grown and had left home before I was born. Wood had graduated from medical school and was an ear, eye, nose, and throat specialist on the staff of the Tennessee Coal and Iron hospital in Birmingham. It humiliated him that Daddy insisted on buying reading glasses at the drugstore instead of getting prescription glasses from him.

Jamie was married and had two daughters. Sing (Hazel) and Sugar (Dot). Sing, the eldest daughter, was my niece but she was a month younger than me. Jamie was the only one of my siblings who did not go to college and he was the only person in the whole family connection to become a millionaire.

WILSON ALSO GOT in trouble one day when he was supposed to be watching me.

The rambling frame house with its unplanned ells and porches where I grew up in Thomasville was on a hill above the lumberyard and the railroad. We had a grand view of much of the town including the bank where Daddy worked.

One day Daddy called Mother and asked, "Where is Kathryn?"

"She is in the backyard playing with Wilson," Mother replied.

"You'd better go see," Daddy said.

When she went outside, Mother saw Wilson, his dogs, and me walking back and forth on the very top of the house. I was maybe three years old. Mother had what my nephew later called "a committee fit."

THOSE REMINISCENCES ARE examples of how *She* and I spend our time now that I am within scratching distance of my ninety-third birthday. Between recalling memories, cooking, napping, taking medicine, and otherwise looking after *She*, there is not even an hour to spare for what I want to do!

I do know that nothing is right since *She* arrived. I used to fix good, nutritious breakfasts of bacon, eggs, crunchy toast or waffles and orange juice. Not anymore. Takes too long. Takes even longer to chew!

"Your cooking is becoming simpler and simpler," *She* complains.

"I notice you're still eating it!"

One of my simplest meals is sausage balls browned in an iron skillet, drained, and put in an oven-proof container with apple butter (not apple sauce) poured over them and heated until the apple butter is bubbling. With a green salad and crunchy bread, that one dish makes a satisfactory meal. So does a small baked potato stuffed with sharp cheese.

Dessert? No more pies and cakes. Maybe ice cream from the grocery store, but more likely a treat some friend has provided. I still favor a simple concoction from childhood: saltine crackers with marshmallows on them, run into the oven until the marshmallows are lightly toasted.

I also confess that I am an Eagle Brand condensed milk addict. I keep at least one can in my refrigerator and eat it with a spoon. My high school friend Lyles Carter Walker used to boil a can of condensed milk for four hours, let it cool and then roll it in crushed pecans. Oh, it was good! But I like it just as well plain and cold out of the refrigerator.

Also from childhood, I like a bowl of cornbread and milk for supper, with fresh fruit for dessert.

"You are so old you can't remember but two ingredients for a recipe," *She* said.

"Some excellent recipes have only two ingredients," I replied. "You seem to like well enough a bowl of sliced bananas with orange juice poured over them."

She couldn't say anything to that.

She TAKES NAPS

I know I spend too much time cooking, eating, and cleaning up after each meal, but everything takes so much time these days. If I didn't have to provide *She*'s meals, I would have plenty of time—well, maybe not plenty, but much more. There would even be more time for naps. Taking naps is one thing *She* and I do not quarrel about.

Naps are a tradition in my family. When I was growing up, Daddy used to take a short nap after dinner (midday) each day before he walked back to his office. Everything in the household was still and quiet while Daddy slept for ten minutes. I can still hear our cook, Thurza, out in the backyard threatening to wring the neck of any hen that squawked or any rooster that crowed while Mr. Jim was taking a nap.

On Sunday afternoons, after Sunday school,

church, and a big dinner, everybody in our family took a long nap. I did not often go to sleep, but I used the quiet time to memorize all the stanzas of a hymn in the *Hymnal* of the Methodist Episcopal Church, South, or a whole chapter in the King James Version Bible—Daddy gave me that weekly assignment.

(As a result, I seldom needed a hymn book at church through the years, and I can still quote scripture with the best of them. Now, when I worry or get upset, *She* often reminds me of one of those passages of comforting scripture.)

HAVING GROWN UP in the sensible Southern tradition of taking a nap after dinner, I have always been aware of the benefits of ten or fifteen minutes of complete relaxation. As a child, I watched Negro men napping on the platform of the freight depot by the railroad, moving to sunny sheltered spots on chilly days and seeking the shade in the summer.

I also watched worshippers at our church nap during the sermon. Five members of our congregation fell asleep every Sunday morning, and I would entertain myself by betting in what order they would nod off. I laughed to myself at the absurdity of grown people falling asleep in public.

And now, *She* does it. Or *She* would if we still went to church. I can't recall exactly when it started, but some time ago I noticed that *She* was getting drowsy during the sermon, fighting to hold her eyes open. A few times, *She* actually drifted off. And once, to the amusement of people around us, her purse slid from her lap and clattered to the floor. It wasn't that the sermons were boring (we were blessed with an excellent preacher), but *She* just couldn't keep her eyes open. I wanted to poke her and whisper what my Aunt Bet used to say, "If you hold one foot about an inch off the floor, you won't go to sleep." I knew from experience, however, that is only a short-term solution.

She finally confessed to being so fearful of going so soundly asleep that she would topple over into the lap of a pew-sharer, or, even worse, slide under the pew in front of us and have to be hauled up off the floor. The possibilities for disaster were frightening. So we quit going to church.

I miss this habit of a long lifetime, miss being with my friends there, miss the music, miss counting the organ pipes, miss the sermon, miss the rituals of worship, miss watching the patterns of light on the stained-glass windows, miss the surge of memories that wash over me whenever I enter the sanctuary.

I'm not sure *She* comprehends what she has deprived me of.

SINCE I WAS no longer attending church, I decided to follow our minister's suggestion and read the Bible from cover to cover, Genesis to Revelation. No passages of literature are more beautiful than the King James Version of the scriptures, but I chose a modern translation, The Book, because it is easier to read.

I started with the New Testament, and it was a joy to read those familiar passages, though, as usual, Revelation left me puzzled. The Old Testament wasn't so easy. I found many stories that I had known since childhood, but some stories were new to me. I had never heard them in my Methodist Sunday School classes. The long begats and most of the prophets gave me trouble, almost caused me to abandon the project.

I was relieved when I got to Daniel. The story of Daniel and the lion's den was like reuniting with an old friend. Unfortunately, nothing else in the book is as exciting as that story.

I was sitting at my dining room table dutifully reading Daniel out loud to *She* when sleep suddenly engulfed her. *She* fell forward and banged her head on the pine table. Hard.

Almost immediately *She* had a big knot on her forehead and a black eye. I know nobody believed me when in answering their inquiries I told them *She* had been injured while reading Daniel. But when the swelling went down, *She* and I had a big private laugh about it.

She REMINDED ME of other nap stories. There was this merchant in southwest Alabama who sold everything in his country store from coffins to horse collars. The coffins were in a small display area on the second floor of the store—except one that he kept behind the counter near the cash register. That was the coffin he had chosen to be buried in. Every afternoon after dinner he took a nap in his coffin. Many a customer entering the store, seeing no one and calling out "Is anybody here?" was startled to see a sleepy man rise up out of a coffin!

I don't nap in it, but I already have my own coffin, a handmade beauty that cost me $250, out in the storage shed behind the garage. I've had it waiting since I turned seventy. The Bible spoke of a lifetime of three score years and ten and I wanted to be prepared, so I asked John Moss to make me a simple pine box, complete with rope handles, and he did. John is a master craftsman and my coffin is a masterpiece. I am not in a hurry to use it, but I am ready. Meanwhile, it is a good storage spot for things I value but don't need every day, like the good set of china.

Many people avoid talking about death, but it

has never bothered me. The principal of my high school, Professor George Harris, taught our eleventh grade American History class. He was an excellent teacher. One day he was writing on the blackboard when he suddenly turned around and said, "Life is a great adventure and death is the greatest adventure of all," then went back to the board.

I have never feared death since then.

A few years ago, when I pointed out to my doctor that all my physical woes are associated with aging, he replied, "You are not old! You're just on the outer fringes of middle age."

We both laughed. But no one can tell us how far these fringes extend. Now as I have gotten established in my nineties, I know I am very close to the end of those fringes. Yes, Professor Harris, life has indeed been an adventure, and now I am ready for the greatest adventure of all.

BEFORE *She* TOOK over so much of my life, I used to take proper naps, fifteen to twenty-five minutes in the afternoon. No longer. *She* likes naps and is not addicted to moderation. To keep peace in the household, I join in her long naps. It is not unusual for us to sleep two or three hours in the afternoon.

The starting time does not matter. We can fall sound asleep in three minutes anytime or anywhere. Disruptions do not annoy us. I can answer the telephone, carry on a conversation, and immediately go back to sleep. In fact, it has gotten to the point that if we do not have a nap, *She* becomes irritable and cross.

Long afternoon naps do not interfere at all with my sleep at night. No matter how long we sleep in the afternoon or what time *She* lets me get to bed at night, sleep comes as soon as I stretch out in bed, and I sleep soundly (except for a trip to the bathroom) until my alarm or a telephone call wakes me.

I now spend too much time sleeping, wasting many hours, but *She* rebels at the idea of cutting back. When I ask my doctor about it, he grins and says that if we could bottle up and sell my sleep secret, we'd be millionaires before dark.

I Cope, *She* Laughs

For years before *She* took up residence, I walked at least a mile a day, usually picking up trash as I walked. *She* does not like to walk and can come up with all manner of excuses not to go outside the house—too hot, too chilly, raining, looks like it might rain, somebody might come to see us, knee hurts, need new walking shoes, etc., etc.

She finds it amusing that I try to make up for the loss of outdoor exercise by goose-stepping through the house: out of the kitchen, through the dining room, down the hall, through a bedroom and bath, down the hall again to the living room and den, back to the kitchen, to finally circuit the family room, all the while mimicking Hitler's high-stepping storm troopers.

Recently my doctor suggested that the upper part of my body needed exercise, too, that I should use weights to strengthen my arms. When I informed him that I had no weights or dumbbells and did not plan to buy any, he laughed and said, "Then just hold a can of soup in each hand. That will work fine."

So now *She* watches me marching through the house waving a cream of celery soup in one hand and chicken noodle in the other. After a few circuits, I collapse from fatigue and *She* collapses from laughter.

At first I did not associate age with my inability to open those small packages of cookies or crackers doled out by airplane attendants. Then I began to notice that passengers all around me were able to tear the plastic wrappings off their snacks with very little difficulty. While I was still struggling to "lift here" or to punch a hole in the plastic with my fingernails, my traveling companions had finished their snacks and returned to reading or to listening to whatever they listened to on earphones or playing electronic games or working their computers. It would be so easy to slit the wrapping with a pen knife or scissors, but those weapons are no longer allowed on flights. The seemingly indestructible packaging makes me yearn for the pre-plastic days: paper is much easier to deal with than the modern miracle wrappings.

I used to struggle a long time before asking my seat mate for help. Now, older and wiser, I don't hesitate to ask, "Would you please open this for me?" The request is dealt with in seconds. I say, "Thank you." My helper replies, "No problem." (Sadly, that will be our longest conversation on a flight that may last for hours. We humans have almost forgotten how to talk to each other. The recorded voices of strangers fill our lives.)

There are problems with opening things at home, too. At the grocery, I try to remember to ask the bag boy to loosen the caps on jars of pickles and relishes before I leave the store. And there are the homemade jellies and preserves those friends bring me. I have assorted gadgets that are supposed to open all kinds of containers, but they don't work for me. *She* finds my struggles highly entertaining, and I resist pointing out that I face these challenges on her account.

I'm just glad I don't have to go to school. I read not long ago that a child should be able to open a milk carton easily before starting to school. In recent years, I've never met the milk carton that I could open without a hacksaw.

Buttons deserve several paragraphs of complaints, but I will only report that *She* laughs at my fumbling fingers, while I praise the inventors of Velcro, zippers, and snaps.

Prescription bottles and other drugstore products give me the most trouble. I have been trading with Selma's Carter Drug Company for nearly seven decades. They know I have no small children—or children of any age—in my house, but they insist on putting my pills and capsules in child-proof, round green plastic bottles which I cannot open. The instructions are simple enough: press down on the top and turn. No matter how hard I press down or how hopefully I turn, no tops come off. I long for the good old days of cork stoppers. I expected changes when I threatened not to pay for any prescription I couldn't open. That seemed fair to me, but alas the pill bottles remain aging-adult-proof.

For years my medicine cabinet contained only toothbrushes, toothpaste, deodorant, Vicks salve, and such. It never, not even when my three children were growing up, held even a laxative or antacid.

The sparse number of my medications must have troubled *She* because soon after she arrived, round pill bottles from Carter's began to multiply. I cannot pronounce their names nor do I know what they are supposed to correct or cure. At last count, seventeen of those green plastic bottles were huddled together in my medicine cabinet.

"Why are you taking so much medicine?" *She* asked.

"Because of you," I replied testily. "I never had to take any until you arrived."

Last year I had so many green pill bottles that I decided *She* and I would decorate our Christmas tree with them. I used a heated ice pick (found in my tool drawer) to punch holes in the tops and bottoms of scores of containers so I could string them on red ribbon with a red bead between each bottle. They made a lovely garland. Getting the labels off the bottles was the most time-consuming part of the process. I plan to start soaking them earlier this year. The garland itself was free, but at one point I began calculating how much money the bottles on it represented—the figure made me sick, so I quit.

Carter's is a remarkable drugstore: they still allow local charge accounts and they deliver and their varied stock of non-medical merchandise is amazing. Even *She* is impressed. I can telephone an order for household products I need, and before I know it the items are at my kitchen door.

Not long ago, I needed a prescription refilled (another bottle for the garland) so I called Carter's. When I dialed the number, a strange tone came over the phone. I figured I had misdialed, so I tried again. The same thing happened. After the third time getting the unpleasant noise instead of the pleasant "This is Carter's, how may I help you," I was frustrated and angry. What was the problem with my trusted drugstore? I muttered some bad words I have learned from *She*.

Then I looked hard at the green cylinder that I wanted refilled. The truth hit me: I was dialing the prescription number!

She laughed about that one for days, and since then has been nagging me every time I start to make a telephone call—even to family or friends whose numbers I have known for years—to check the number in the directory just to make sure.

The story about my dialing the prescription number has amused not just *She* but many people. Some laugh because they can't imagine doing it themselves. Others laugh because they have done similar things or can easily see how they could. Either way, they laugh.

How can old people survive without laughter? One of my mature friends prays daily, "God please keep me from falling, but if I do fall, please let me be able to tell about it and laugh." I pray the same prayer.

Of course, I was calling Carter's because I couldn't drive myself there as I had been doing for more than sixty years. Soon after my ninety-first birthday, I drove to see my eye doctor, an attractive woman so young it couldn't have been many years ago that she was playing doctor with her dolls.

The young doctor gave my eyes a thorough examination and then asked, "Who drove you here?" When I told her that I had driven myself, her reply was, "Please drive carefully on your way home. You should not be driving. It's not safe for you or for other motorists. Your lack of peripheral vision makes it unsafe for you to drive."

She was not surprised by the doctor's decision. "I've been afraid to ride with you for years!" she told me.

"Then why do you insist on going everywhere I go?" I asked. "As I recall, you often suggest that we go visit friends, or ride out to see new houses in Valley Grande or to count the potholes on Church Street. Now we are housebound. We can't go anywhere."

"Being housebound will be good for you," *She*

replied. "It will teach you patience and how to do without and how to get organized. You need to make lists."

Patience is not easily practiced when dealing with a self-righteous old woman. For one thing, I learned to do without during the Great Depression. My father used to say about doing without: "Do like the Hindu. Do the best you kindu. If you ain't got no clothes make your skindu."

THUS ENDED A long driving career covering hundreds upon hundreds of thousands of miles, a career during which I never received a single ticket for traffic violations.

I did have a few close calls. A few years ago driving up in north Alabama I realized I was about to be late for a speaking engagement. I sped up. Traffic was light and time was passing. I sped up some more. Then I saw blue lights coming toward me. I pulled over and had my driver's license in my hand when the young (everybody is young when you reach my age) state trooper came up to my car. He looked at my license and said, "Mrs. Windham!" in a reproachful tone. "You told me stories when I was in the fourth grade. Now you slow down."

I did, grateful for a narrow escape.

Of all the deprivations of aging, having to give up driving is one of the most difficult. It proclaims loss of independence and you dread the inevitable impositions on good friends.

Seeing my old Valiant with its State of Alabama-issued "Jeffrey" vanity license plate on the bumper and more than 100,000 miles on its odometer sitting forlornly in the driveway makes me sad. I hid the ignition key in a desk drawer so I wouldn't be tempted to drive again.

I Forget, *She* Smirks

Since I have lost the convenience of driving, I depend on younger friends to take me shopping. Being dependent on other people irks me.

"It's all your fault," I tell *She*. "All your fault."

"I suppose being ninety-two years old has nothing to do with your inability to drive," *She* retorts. "Seems to me that at your age you should have learned to accept help graciously. It's high time you learned that simple courtesy."

Her delight in her own perfection irks me.

She irritates me further by losing the shopping lists I make. I am an excellent, even expert list maker. I have made them for years. The lists I make for the grocery store include everything I could possibly need until someone else volunteers to take me shopping again. I try not to waste my friends' time.

Unfortunately, my lists not only get lost but

too often I cannot decipher my own writing. "Poor penmanship is your own fault," *She* tells me. "You never did have pretty handwriting, not even in the third grade when you had to make rows and rows of flowing circles and other rows of smooth, even, between-the-lines up and down strokes. You just can't write!"

That got off with me, so I snapped back, "I wrote so well I could hold three pencils in my right hand and, staying neatly in the lines, write 'I will not talk in school' one hundred times so I could go out and play at recess. Do you know anybody else who could do that?"

"Huh!? Three pencils at once!" And *She* flounced off, muttering about handwriting. I hate it when *She* gets preachy.

On the lists that I do find and can read I am still unaccustomed to seeing "disposable underpants." *She* is to blame for that addition, too.

As all her annoyances do, this one started out simply. I was just beginning to become aware of her presence in my life when I began having sudden urges to go to the bathroom. The occasions on which I did not reach my goal in time gradually increased. I dealt with this embarrassing development by resorting to the use of sanitary pads, a nuisance I had not had to deal with since menopause.

I had advanced to the "super absorbent" category when I had a long hospital/rehab stay early in 2011 for an illness that had nothing to do with my bladder.

During my rehabilitation, a strange and annoying thing happened with my memory. "Give My Regards to Broadway," the Lord's Prayer, and the 23rd Psalm became entangled in my mind.

Before I could get rid of one, another took its place. How "Give My Regards to Broadway" got involved, I will never understand, but these three memory fragments continuously intertwined themselves in my mind. They woke me up at night.

I tried pushing them aside by humming or singing other songs, but nothing worked. Nothing.

"You are just crazy," *She* told me. I hope not.

Memory is a funny thing. Some people never forget a face, others can remember both the faces and the names that go with them. Some politicians and salespeople are especially known for this trait. I don't know if they are born that way or learn it because they are ambitious.

For myself, I have always liked all sorts of poetry and found it easy to memorize, from Burma Shave rhymes to the British poem about "that orbed maiden with white fire laden." I do not agree with Dorothy Parker who said, "I'd rather flunk my Wasserman test than read the poetry of Edgar Guest." Nobody remembers now what a Wasserman test was and maybe that is a good thing.

No poetry anywhere is more beautiful than the Psalms. I'm grateful that I learned some so many years ago.

She considers learning poetry a waste of time. *She* accuses me of being high-faluting in my choice of poetry.

"You have never advanced beyond 'Mary Had a Little Lamb,' " I tell her, "and you probably don't even know the second verse of that poem."

She quickly tried to change the subject but I went on by reciting Carl Sandburg's sad little poem:

> *No memory of having starred*
> *Makes up for later disregard*
> *Or keeps the end*
> *From being hard.*

WHEN I WAS a child, Mother used to read to me the poems in Robert Louis Stevenson's *A Child's Garden of Verses*. I liked the rhythm of his stanzas and the pictures he created with words.

I could recite nearly all of them by heart. I still can. Somehow, *She* reminds me of one of his poems:

> *My Shadow*
>
> *I have a little shadow that goes in and out with*
> *me,*
> *And what can be the use of her is more than I can*
> *see.*

She is very, very like me from her heels up to the
head;
And I see her jump before me when I jump into
my bed.

The part about the bed does not apply to *She* and
me. We no longer jump into bed.

Another childhood poetry memory involves
the Thomasville post office. Before the days of city
mail delivery, the post office lobby was the most
popular place in town after the passenger/mail train
ran. People gathered there to get their mail, to visit
with friends, to learn the latest gossip. Teenagers met
there to make dates and plan their activities.

Thomasville had no funeral homes, so notices
of white residents' funeral services were posted in
black frames in the post office lobby. There was a
different tradition for black residents: the church
at Choctaw Corner tolled the bell when a member
died. After the initial tolling, the bell was rung once
for each year in the deceased person's life. In those

quiet times, it could be heard all over Thomasville. It was a loving, dignified custom.

Back then crates of baby chicks were shipped by mail, and they could often be heard peeping in the back of the post office as they awaited their new owner.

My Aunt Bet was the postmaster and during the summer, she bought and cut a watermelon for the staff every afternoon on a big table in the back of the post office.

Aunt Bet refused to be called "postmistress." "I am nobody's mistress," she declared. "I am the postmaster." And she was.

My own first public performance was in Aunt Bet's post office lobby. *She* says I was two years old, but I am not sure. The lobby was full of people. Aunt Bet or cousin Tabb stood me on the ledge of the stamp window, and I recited:

I'm a cute little girl
With a cute little figger:
Stand back, boys, until

I Forget, She Smirks

I get a little bigger.

ONE OF THE first things I saw every morning when I was growing up was part of a poem by Grace Noll Crowell that my mother had typed out and put in the corner of the mirror of my dressing table. I read it every morning while I combed my hair.

New Day

> *This day will bring some lovely thing,*
> *I say it o'er with each new dawn,*
> *Some bright, adventurous thing to hold against*
>   *my heart*
> *And treasure after it is gone.*
> *And so I rise to greet*
> *The day with wings upon my feet.*

Nor do I know who wrote one of my favorite poems. It fell out of my sister Annelee's Bible when I was looking up a passage one day. I know she did not write it.

Life is like a journey on a train
With passengers sitting at each window pane.
We may sit far apart the whole journey through.
You may never know me, I may never know you.
But if, by chance, we sit side by side
Let's be pleasant companions—'tis so short a ride.

Then there are Jan Struther's words from her poem "Eulogy":

She was twice blessed:
She was happy; She knew it.

I want those sentences on my tombstone.

She Is Slow

The most aggravating change *She* has made in my life, I suppose, is how she has slowed me down. Everything takes longer to do now, two or three times as long, even as simple a task as making a cup of instant coffee.

Julia Tutwiler, whom I greatly admire, used to tell the young ladies in her classes at Livingston University, "A wife should be able to dress attractively in ten minutes to accompany her husband to any gathering." Miss Julia, it should be noted, never married. She prescribed the same doctrine, though allowing a bit more time, about putting good meals on the table.

I never lived completely up to Miss Julia's speedy standards, but I was never late to any class when I was in school or to any meeting or appointment when I got older. Looking back on it, I think I wasted a lot of time being on time.

There was the time when I was in grammar school and our house caught on fire. It was right after breakfast when a passer-by saw flames on our wood-shingled roof.

Neighbors responded quickly, as did grown-ups in our family. Almost immediately there were men on the roof dousing the flames with buckets of water from the well on our back porch.

Meanwhile, I, seven years old, looked at the clock on the mantel in my parents' bedroom and saw that school time was fast approaching, so I gathered up my pencil and tablet and ran toward school.

I never once looked back toward our house until I joined the line of pupils waiting to march into class. The school was on a hill, across the railroad tracks and on the other end of town, a mile from home, and our house was also on a hill, so I had a good view.

I could see no smoke in the direction of our house, so I figured it had not burned.

The important thing was that I was not late to school.

THOUGH I HAVE an aversion to being late, I do not like to be hurried. When I married Amasa, the only advice my mother gave him was, "Kathryn has a good disposition, is easy to get along with most of the time, but don't ever try to hurry her, and don't ever try to make up a bed with her."

Amasa laughed and evidently took to heart half of her advice—in our too-brief years of marriage, he never even offered to help me make up a bed.

BEING SLOW IS a major hindrance that has steadily worsened since *She* moved in. For instance, the telephone rings, and before my stiff knees can get me to it, the caller has hung up, hung up after only four or five rings. Anybody over eighty years old should be given the courtesy of at least eight or nine rings before the caller hangs up. Patience, *She* tells me, is a fast-disappearing virtue.

Resting, I tell *She*, is another virtue and is not to

be confused with being slow. It upsets *She* for me to sit still even for a few minutes.

"Don't you know you have work to do? What are you doing now?"

"Twiddling my thumbs. Maybe I should teach you how. If you have enough sense to shoo the chickens, you should be able to twiddle your thumbs. Once I teach you how to do it frontwards, you can try to learn to twiddle backwards," I told her.

She was not amused.

Twiddling is a nearly lost pleasure, right along with scraping soot from the back of the fireplace with a poker or counting the cars on a train.

She claims she has always known how to count and how to read. I doubt it. *She* laughs when I say I learned to count by counting the boxcars on the train that rolled past on the Southern railroad below our home. I could stand on our front porch and count the long train of cars.

Railroads were important to me and my family. In bitterly cold weather, we judged the severity of the cold by the length of the icicles hanging from the big green water tank between the tracks behind the depot, and in the hot summer it was always cool and damp under the tank. Thick, green moss flourished there, perfect for carpeting doll playhouses between the roots of trees.

On those rare, restless nights when sleep refused to come, it was comforting to hear the midnight freight stop at the water tank and then roll on towards Mobile.

Even more comforting was hearing my father knock the ashes from his pipe against the fireplace in his bedroom—telling me that someone else was awake, someone who loved me.

Daddy and I often watched trains from our front porch. Back in the 1920s when we saw flat cars loaded with scrap iron on their way to Japan, Daddy said, "That is not good. One day that metal will come back to us in another form."

When the first chain store opened in Thomasville, the Yellow Front Store, Daddy said, "That is not good. Chain stores will put all the small mom and pop stores out of business."

SHE

How did he know those things?

And how do I remember them now? That is one good thing about having *She* around. While I may have some trouble remembering what I am doing today, I can count on *She* to remember what I was doing eighty or ninety years ago.

She Electrifies Me

My evolution into an electronic woman began simply enough after *She* arrived. At first, it did not even involve electric power, just a simple walking cane.

As I moved toward my ninth decade, my good doctor told me that he would be more comfortable if I walked with a cane. So when my friend and neighbor Charlie Lucas (the Tin Man) brought me a cane he had found in a trash pile, I promised to use it—when I remembered and when I could find it. It is a plain cane but unusually light and strong. Nobody can tell me what kind of wood it is made of. Gradually, I came to rely on the cane and to feel unsteady without it.

For years I have had problems about going down steps. I could climb steps forever, but fear of falling,

I suppose, seized me when I looked down. I needed just a little support.

This phobia has become worse since *She* moved in with me. Now I am afraid to do so simple a thing as to step off the sidewalk into the street. *She* laughs at me about that.

In 2008, when I was still able to drive, I needed to mail a package, so I drove to the post office and parked. Halfway across the parking lot, I realized I had forgotten my cane, the reassurance I would need when I had to step off the sidewalk on my return to the car.

But I went on in, because I was sure there would be someone in the lobby to help me. Wouldn't you know the lobby was deserted, not one single soul there.

I walked out to the curb and looked at that six-inch step to the street. "You surely can make that little step safely," I told myself. "Don't be foolishly afraid of such a little thing." But I was.

I stood there several minutes hoping someone would come to my rescue but no one did. The only living person I saw was a black man across the street, so I called, "Would you please come help me?" He let me put my hand on his shoulder when I stepped down, then he walked to the car with me, opened the door, got me settled, and signaled when it was safe to back out.

I leaned out the window and thanked him. "I thank you for asking me," he replied.

I DIDN'T IMMEDIATELY associate *She* with the arrival and use of that cane. Nor did I think to blame her at first when I replaced the high double bed that I had been sleeping in for decades, one that I almost had to take a running jump to get into at night. The old iron bed had decorative touches of a craftsman's art. I saw it leaning against the side of a barn in rural Wilcox County years ago and bought it for fifteen dollars. My new bed cost considerably more.

The new bed was necessary because even I had become fearful that I might fall, especially after I made one of my nightly pilgrimages to the bathroom.

Now I can sit on the side of my new bed with

my feet on the floor. "It is not as attractive as my old bed was, but it is safer," I tell *She* when she complains about how it spoils the look of the room.

She grudgingly admitted I had a point. "If you fall out of this low, tacky bed, you won't get hurt," *She* said. "Dilcy and Ben started to put you on a trundle bed or a soft pallet. But they'd never be able to get you up off the floor from a pallet, and a trundle bed wouldn't be that much better."

Anyhow, I haven't seen a trundle bed in years.

THERE WERE OTHER non-electronic changes in my lifestyle, but I still was not fully aware how *She* was taking over. *She* is a subtle creature.

The installation of a high commode in my bathroom was a real comfort. Several of my elderly friends had high commodes installed in their baths after they tried mine.

Magnifying glasses came next. All my life I have liked to read, but since *She*'s arrival reading is a struggle. Words run together, the type is too small, there is not enough contrast between the paper and the ink. The truth is that ninety-two year-old eyes are worn out.

She claimed not to understand my addiction to reading. "If you had not read so much, your eyes would not be worn out," *She* informed me.

"You'd better be glad my sight is failing," I replied. "If I could read, I'd be deep in a book instead of taking care of you!"

THAT EPISODE SOLIDIFIED my awareness that my life would henceforth be controlled by my uninvited guest.

The electronic takeover began with the arrival of a highly recommended reading lamp. The lamp had a long, flexible neck to make it easy to focus on pages or words where additional light was needed. It also had a long cord.

All appliances have cords. In due time, a tangle of electrical cords invaded my house like kudzu. *She* predicted that I was going to catch my foot in a cord, fall down and break both hips. I feared the same fate.

Warnings of falling echoed in every room: "Watch out for these cords! Don't trip over the cords! Be careful where you step!" pretty much replaced conversation around our house.

One of those cords was attached to a large recliner that works by electricity to lift your feet, place you in a reclining position, or even stand you up. It is an amazing piece of furniture, sort of a hybrid between a lounge chair and a hospital bed. I already had a recliner that worked by a manual lever on the side. I had enjoyed many wonderful naps in that recliner, but it was difficult to operate. My new recliner operated with the press of a button. It was simple, efficient, and comfortable.

I was amazed by that chair and enjoyed demonstrating and showing it off. "I have been sentenced to the electric chair," I joked with visitors who had not already seen it. At least I was not attached to the chair's cord. All I had to do was avoid being tripped up by it.

THAT CHAIR WAS my final encounter with relative

freedom. Since then I've been almost completely tethered.

First came the oxygen. It arrived with a tank and a cord (of course) and a clear tube with little bumps on it to go into my nostrils and loops for fastening around each ear to hold it in place. My orders were to wear it when I sleep, including naps, and exercise. When I complained about it, *She* said, "You're ninety-two. What did you expect?"

I got the same response when I complained about the breathing machine they brought to clear my lungs, another machine with more electrical cords.

Another major step in my conversion into Electronic Woman came when my electric stockings arrived, with one cord attached to each leg and a long cord to plug into the wall outlet.

There was hardly anywhere to step without risking tripping and falling or pulling loose a plug. Double sockets were everywhere, and wherever I might be sitting or lying, I was attached to one of the cords.

She found this amusing. I didn't.

"It's all your fault," I fumed. "Everything was fine until you joined our family. It is all your fault!"

She was so interested in the electrical stockings that she failed to reply. Those appliances wrapped around each leg, expanding and deflating in rhythm. They are engineered to squeeze excess fluid out of the legs.

"Do they expect a phoenix to rise from this nest of electrical cords?" I asked.

She didn't answer.

She AND FENG SHUI

Neither *She* nor I can pronounce or spell that Chinese art of interior decorating, but *She* endorses it wholeheartedly.

"We've got to do something about all this stuff in this house, got to get rid of most of it," *She* told me.

"It was here before you came," I reminded her.

"There's more of it now," *She* retorted.

I couldn't deny that accusation.

"We'll start by throwing out that plaster leg in the family room," *She* said.

"Never! Never! Never!"

Yes, there is a plaster leg in one corner of the family room. Admittedly it is a rather unusual decorative item, perhaps because it looks so real. It is flesh-colored and even has varicose veins. I laugh to myself when I see visitors staring at it or taking quick, repeated glances at it. If they don't have enough curiosity to ask, I never tell them anything and they leave my house thinking I am even more peculiar than they thought.

Actually, that leg has a story, as does nearly everything in my house. When I was a little girl and annoyed him, my brother Wilson—thirteen years older than me—used to threaten to jerk my leg off and beat me over the head with the bloody end.

Over the years, I often repeated Wilson's mock warning to my children and grandchildren. The expression became part of our family lore.

I don't know where he found it, but one Christmas my grandson Ben Hilley, then a teenager, gave me that leg as a present. His friends were shocked at his choice of a gift. "Surely you are not going to give that thing to your grandmother for Christmas," they said.

"Yes, I am," Ben replied, "and she will love it."

And I did. That leg will remain in my house for as long as I do. *She* understands that now.

She ALSO WANTED me to get rid of the photographs that line the hallway walls.

"You don't even know who most of those people are," *She* claims, but I do.

She professed not to believe a word of the unusual story associated with one of those photographs, but it is true, every word of it.

Back in the 1940s, when I was a reporter for the *Birmingham News*, I was assigned to cover a big deer hunt honoring Governor Chauncey Sparks at the Bull Pen Hunting Club at a remote site near Sunflower in southwest Alabama. Writers from several publications covered the event, and photos from the hunt hang on the hallway wall.

In the early 2000s, a photographer who was born in Russia, educated in Alabama, and had a photographic business in Huntsville spent several months in and around Selma photographing the Black Belt. The region fascinated him.

One day he came to my house to interview me. When he arrived, I asked a few basic questions in an effort to know and feel comfortable with him. "How did you get interested in photography?"

"My grandfather was a photographer, and he left me his cameras. He worked for *Life*."

That was interesting.

Still asking casual, polite questions, I said, "What was his name?"

"William Shrout."

I broke out in goosebumps. "Your grandfather's picture is hanging on the wall right down that hall," I told my visitor.

Sure enough, the picture shows his grandfather and me at the Bull Pen Hunting Club, standing in front of several deer carcasses hanging from a sturdy line. Their antlers nearly scrape the ground.

Around William Shrout's neck is a camera, the very camera Boris was using at my house that day, the gift from his grandfather. He used it to photograph the picture of his grandfather, a family treasure he happened upon in Selma, Alabama.

No pictures are leaving that wall.

However, once *She* gets her mind set on a project,

it is about impossible to distract her. *She* continued to obsess about removing some photographs from my hallway gallery.

"What are all those children dressed up like grown folks?" *She* asked, pointing to a large photograph of what looked like a wedding party.

"That is a Tom Thumb wedding," I told her.

"What? A wedding with first and second graders in it? Stupidest thing I ever heard of. Did you think it up?"

"No, I did not think it up. And it is not stupid. Tom Thumb weddings once raised lots of money for the PTA and church groups. Wouldn't you pay a dime or a quarter to see your child or grandchild or a neighbor's child in a wedding? I was in that wedding, and lots of my family and friends came. I'm the one with the big bow in her hair."

"I see you aren't the bride. I bet that didn't set well with you," *She* laughed.

To be truthful, I had been upset. The groom was Bittie Griffin, the cutest boy I knew. He and I were deskmates in the first grade. I hated seeing him married to Nan Claire Grantham, whose father was the railroad station agent. He had a big flower garden between the railroad tracks behind the depot. It was the only beauty spot in downtown Thomasville, but that gave her no right to be the bride.

I could not look when, after Bittie and Nan Claire had repeated the wedding vows and the child playing the preacher had pronounced them man and wife, they kissed.

THE HALLWAY GALLERY isn't the only area where *She* and I have had decorating discord. I like photographs on my refrigerator door. *She* says they are tacky, just a step above trailer trash. "But each picture has a story," I tell her. "Even the photo of the sign of that cheap motel."

More than half a century ago, after I had published my first book of ghost stories, WSFA-TV in Montgomery interviewed me. I had never seen myself on television and was eager to do so. I had spoken in Troy the day the interview was televised, so I thought I would drive back to Montgomery to

Martha and Allen Rankin's home in time to see it.
However, I was late leaving Troy and realized I could
not get there in time. I decided to stop at a motel and
watch the TV in the lobby instead. When I entered
the lobby of the Pine Needle Motel, several men
were watching a baseball game. I knew they would
not change channels to watch me, so I arranged to
rent a room for an hour. The baseball fans appeared
to be interested in that transaction.

I watched my interview and return to the lobby
to hand the clerk the room key. On my way out, I
heard one man say, "And he never came." Another
added, "And she even paid!"

That photo will stay on my refrigerator no matter
what *She* says.

BEFORE *She* INTRUDED, unexpected and uninvited,
into my life and decided to take up interior decorating, I knew where every piece of furniture, every
electrical appliance was. I could walk through the
house in complete darkness and know precisely
where I was.

Not anymore. Much of the house has been rear-ranged, "for comfort and safety."

One of the major changes is in the living/dining room where the long pine table, the first piece of furniture my husband and I ever bought, has been shoved over against the wall to make a wide path for a walker. Rugs have been rolled and pushed out of the way.

I have a dozen rocking chairs in the house. Each chair has its own story—like the one Aunt Bet won for making the best pound cake at the Clarke County Fair in about 1905—and I knew each story and each location until *She* came. Changes had to be made to keep my walker or cane from getting entangled in protruding legs and rockers.

And anyway, "You don't need to sit down and rock," *She* told me. "You need to be up finishing some of your projects."

"You take more of my time than any project," I replied. She pretended not to hear.

I knew where all the old bookcases were, the glass-front ones from Daddy's office in the Thomasville bank, the shelves that had been built for holding time schedules in the Old Depot office (a gift to me from former Mayor Joe Smitherman after the city took over the depot building), even the small bookcase Daddy bought me at about age four when I demonstrated that I could lift and tote it across the balcony at Dozier Hardware Company.

I'm grateful that my books, even the books of my childhood, have remained in place, but *She* is not impressed. "What difference does it make where all those books are? You can't see well enough to read them anymore."

She can't understand that my regret is that I did not read more.

She Edits My Stories

My own father was the best storyteller I ever knew. I eventually earned my living telling stories, first as a newspaper reporter and later as a book writer and storyteller. Over the years I have known many fine storytellers, both professionals and gifted amateurs. I learned how to tell stories by listening, and Daddy was my first and best teacher.

He could hear a story in the simple acts of ordinary people. In his retellings, common events took on uncommon meaning or humor. Often both.

It was World War II, and the bus to take draftees from Thomasville to their training camp was filled and ready to pull away from the curb by People's Drug Company.

The sidewalks and streets were filled with family members and friends telling the young men goodbye. Among them was Eva Sparks and her five-year-old son, who had come to say farewell to Mr. Sparks. Wiping away her tears, she waved until the bus was out of sight. Then little Nelson Eddie said matter-of-factly, "Well, that's the last of him."

I LOVE THAT story. I love the emotion it evokes of the leavetaking scene, and I love the boy's innocence with the incongruity of what he says.

She has become more and more a stickler for the truth. *She* delights in correcting my stories and writing.

I try to remind her what a wise weekly newspaper editor, George Carlton in Grove Hill, told me years ago: "Don't risk spoiling a story by investigating it too closely."

She is not impressed. *She* hears only what she wants to hear, sees only what she wants to see, and remembers what she wants to remember. *She* is quick to speak up on any subject, apparently with real authority.

"Your memory is terrible," *She* tells me. "I know what really happened."

77

I am not so sure.

According to *She*, I was about two and a half and had been to Sunday School with my parents. Between Sunday School and church, I walked down the hill with Daddy to the depot to visit friends while he waited to get news from the conductor or the train. It seems he forgot to hold my hand or watch me properly.

Just as the train was arriving, I decided to cross the tracks and go back to Mother at the church. I was too small for the engineer to see, and as Mother watched in horror from a window in the church, it appeared that I was going to be killed by the train. At the last second, Mr. Claude Bagburn reached out and snatched me to safety.

I DO RECALL a later brush with death though *She* and I disagree on the details.

Mother and Tabb had taken me to Grove Hill to a small circus. I was six or seven years old. We had seats on the front row, right at ringside.

The final act was for the elephant to show his

strength by pulling a big metal stake out of the ground, but the giant creature could not pull it out. His keeper became agitated and goaded him, and the elephant became angry and unruly. He kept snorting and circling the stob and leaning back to pull.

At one point, his behind was about in my lap. I had never been close to an elephant's rear end before. If the stake had come loose the large animal would have lurched backwards and crushed us.

Right then Mr. Clifton Gilmore, a Grove Hill lawyer, reached down and pulled me to safety.

Later, friends asked Mother, "Weren't you frightened, Helen?" She replied, "No, all I could think about was that my husband would never claim our bodies if we had been sat on by an elephant."

She has different versions of these events. I like mine better.

She SAYS SHE can't believe that I used to play with lizards and June bugs and lightning bugs and such, but I did. Still do.

I miss the green lizards that used to scamper

along the bannister railing of our front porch in Thomasville. "Show me your 'money purse,' " I'd tell them, and they would puff out red sacks under their throats.

June bugs came in the summer when the figs on our trees were ripe. *She* claims she never tied a silk thread to the prickly leg of a June bug so the insect could fly in circles above her head, but I know better—all proper Southern children did.

I also caught doodle bugs. The technique is to spit on a broom straw, get a little dirt on it, poke it down a doodle bug hole in the dry dirt up under the house (our houses then were raised up off the ground; dogs, chickens, and children could wander beneath them) and say, "Doodle bug, doodle bug your house is on fire."

There were bugs of other sorts—and maybe snakes—in the tangle of kudzu in our backyard, but we never minded when we burrowed down in the leaves while playing hide-and-seek. Those kudzu vines provided a fine hiding place.

I remember when Daddy brought those kudzu

vines home in one hand. "The county Extension Service agent gave these to me," he told Mother. "He said they will cover the unsightly coal piles you complain about in the backyard."

They did. Daddy spent the rest of his life trying to get rid of that little handful of kudzu he had planted.

She claims that is not the way it happened but I know it is. One of *She*'s upsetting traits is that she is always so sure she, and only she, is right. *She* is difficult to argue with.

She AND I REMEMBER

Years ago, my young friend Ron Harris and I used to laugh about how his mother would sit on their front porch in Putnam gazing across the pasture for hours.

"What are you doing, Mama?" he would ask.

"Remembering."

Now *She* accuses me of doing the same thing.

"What are you doing sitting there? Remembering?"

"Yes," I tell her.

As I HAVE mentioned, naps are important in my family. Sleep is almost sacred. As a child I was only awakened on special occasions. In the fall or early winter, my father would wake me at night to hear the wild geese fly over Thomasville on their way south.

"Listen," he would say. "Remember. You will never

hear the wild geese when you are grown."

Thurza, our beloved cook, used to wake me to see her Queen of the Night (night-blooming cereus). That plant blooms only once in one hundred years, I have been told, and Thurza did not want me to miss seeing its beauty.

On the summer nights when there were showers of shooting stars, Mother would have a mattress put on the open-air part of our back porch, and she and I would sleep there in the dark. When the stars began shooting, she would awaken me to see that spectacular occurrence beneath the dark night sky. And she would say to me, "The heavens declare the glory of God and the firmament showeth his handiwork."

My most exciting night-awakening was before daylight one fall morning. Daddy came into my room and said, "Get up quickly and dress. We are going to the circus."

"But don't I have to go to school?"

"Not today. We are going to Montgomery to the circus. A real circus!"

I must have dozed when we rode over the hundred and twenty miles of unpaved road to Montgomery but I was wide awake when we reached the big Barnum and Bailey tent on the circus grounds.

I saw Emmett Kelly, the world famous clown, and I watched Lillian Litzel perform on the high trapeze, and I saw the Zucchini Brothers shot from a cannon, and dozens of other acts to stir my imagination and hold in my memory.

Daddy brought me a *papier mâché* bird tied to a string on a big stick. When I whirled the bird around over my head, it sang. I don't know what happened to my singing bird or where you can get one today. I wonder if they all disappeared with the real circuses.

"A real circus," *She* laughs. "That's what your family sounds like to me."

MOTHER'S INSURANCE OFFICE was next door to People's Drug Company and her desk was at a plate glass window at the front. People often came in to visit with her. One day Mr. Hurt stopped by to ask her to "type write" a letter to his granddaughter Velma Rae who was working at the shipyard in Mobile during World War II.

Mother told him she was busy getting out the statements but would be glad to help him the next day.

"The letter needs writing now," he told Mother. "I'm worried about Velma Rae."

Mother tried to reassure him that his granddaughter had been reared properly and was a good girl, but he kept insisting that she needed a letter with his advice.

"Miss Helen, you know how women are weak-willed and easily persuaded."

Mother said that she could not deny his accusation, given that she typed the letter!

I NEVER RAN away from home though I did threaten to become Mr. Alex Hall's child. That was a very strange choice. Mr. Hall was crippled, old and ugly and had a shoe repair business in a small one room building across the street from the Methodist Church.

Dilcy, my youngest child, did leave briefly one night. She packed her little suitcase, went to the front door, flung it open and announced, "I'm going out into the dark and let the mad dogs bite me." She turned around at the end of our walk and came home.

IN THE LIMBS of the tree above the dolls' playhouse was our treehouse that we built ourselves. We found strong, level limbs and nailed boards across them. It was simple, but it was wonderful; it was our own place of refuge that we created for ourselves.

A basket on a rope brought up our supplies: cookies, comic books, rook cards, paper and pencils and such.

When I am shown the treehouses built for today's children, houses with carpeted floors, several kinds of electronic fans, coolers and so on it makes me sad that children have been robbed of the fun and satisfaction of creating their own sanctuaries.

Some towns used to have tree-sitting contests for older children, offering prizes to the person who stayed in a treehouse the longest. One summer my boyfriend Lyles Carter Walker won that contest by staying in his treehouse nearly two weeks. I can't recall what his prize was, something like many boxes of cookies or a hundred ice cream cones, but I know he shared it with me. He got his picture in the Thomasville *Times*. We were all proud of him, but nobody was more pleased than his mother, Miss Cora, who for the first time in his life knew where Lyles Carter was and what he was doing for any period of time.

Years later, in 1976, I knew the pride of being a champion when, to the amazement of my children, my friend Grant Porter and I were the Egg Tossing Champions of Dallas County. We tossed a raw egg back and forth for an incredible distance, completely wiping out our competitors. That achievement was the only championship I ever earned. And Grant and I were not even given plaques.

She and I think it would be interesting and refreshing to revive tree-sitting and egg-tossing.

Uɴᴛɪʟ *She* ᴀʀʀɪᴠᴇᴅ, I had enjoyed good health and vitality, although *She* claims I did get off to a shaky start.

My mother was thirty-six when I was born. Because my father's beloved first wife, Annie, had died of complications following the birth of my brother Wilson, and because Thomasville had no hospital, Daddy sent Mother by train to Selma to Dr. John Furniss's hospital to await my birth.

Mother had a room at the hospital where she waited a month for me to be born. She used to say it was the finest vacation she ever had. She had no responsibilities, so she read, went out to eat with friends, napped, wrote letters, or did handiwork.

I must have been a sickly baby. I heard stories of how Mother put me on a pillow and held me in her arms on train rides to the Selma Baptist Hospital throughout my early childhood. I remember, as I grew older, the endless bowls of cold, gummy oatmeal I was given to eat there. It was seventy years before I ate oatmeal again. I like it now.

Mother did everything she knew to do to keep me healthy. My friends wore bloomers with elastic in the waist, but Mother thought the elastic waist cut off circulation, so my bloomers (they always matched my dress) were buttoned onto what we called a "skeleton waist," which was somewhat like suspenders.

I wore a hat when I played outside on sunny days.

During the summer, my friends could eat watermelon. I could chew it up and swallow the juice, but I had to spit out the pulp.

I could not eat fish until Mother had examined every bite to be certain that no small bones were lurking in it.

At school recess, Mrs. Dave Anderson used to park her car on the edge of the campus and sell candy and popcorn balls. I was not allowed to buy any. Mother fixed me a recess snack of fresh fruit: apples, grapes, peaches, pears, satsumas. I still remember how good those sweet popcorn balls looked.

Thomasville had no water system until I was twelve years old. At school, we drank water from a well; most students drank from a gourd or dipper at the well. I did not. I had my own folding metal cup.

I did go barefoot in the summer after Mother decided the weather was warm enough. However, I could not go barefoot outside until the sun had dried all the dew from the grass. Otherwise, I might get Ground Itch. I had never known anybody with Ground Itch, but I figured it must have been a terrible thing to have, maybe as bad as the Seven Year Itch I had heard the grownups talking about.

At home, especially on the porches, my bare feet were endangered. I occasionally got splinters in my feet. They hurt, and pulling out splinters could be very painful. My cousin Tabb could pull out splinters better than anybody in the family.

While she worked on extracting the splinter, she sometimes sang:

Johnny Boy, who cut your hair?
You say your mother did?
Did she cut it with a meat ax,
You funny looking kid.
Did she freeze it, boy, and break it off?
You know it looks all wrong.
So take my advice if you want to look nice
And Johnny, let your hair grow long.

By the end of the song, Tabb would have extracted the painful splinter. She could also see to pick out redbugs.

I DID NOT start to school until I was seven years old. My friends went to school at age six, but Daddy did not fully approve of the first grade teacher, so he waited for a new teacher for me.

I enjoyed my extra year at home. Among other things, I became expert with my slingshot. We had a big Japanese magnolia tree in our side yard, and bees swarmed to the clusters of yellow flowers.

I gathered up my ammunition of small stones,

stood by the bannister on the side porch, and made war with the bees. I got so expert I could pick out one bee, aim at him and shoot him down. This talent never proved useful in later life.

When I did start to school, I had the best first grade teacher in the world, Miss Carrie Head. Back in those good old days, teachers could hold children in their laps, hug them, blow kisses to them, even spank them if needed without fear of being sued. Miss Head loved every student in her first grade and she told us so.

Even though I was a year late starting school, I had been going to Sunday School for as long as I can remember. On that, at least, *She* does agree with me.

Miss Daisy Clark taught my kindergarten class at the Methodist Church. She was old. To children, all adults seem old. Perhaps my elementary school-aged friend had it right when he told me, "You're not old; you just look old," or my neighbor Charlie Lucas when he said, "Age ain't nothing but numbers."

I do not know.

Miss Daisy had a soft, gentle voice which she never had to raise because we were well-behaved children. After all, our parents were in a Sunday School room right around the corner from us.

But one Sunday we had a visitor, a little boy, who was loud, unruly, disobedient. He pulled books off shelves, turned chairs over, leaned out the window to wave and holler at people passing by.

"Sit down, son," Miss Daisy said to him in her soft voice. "We are having Sunday School." He paid her no attention.

At that point, I rose and said with my five-year-old wisdom, "Let's send him to the Baptists!"

CHILDHOOD RELIGIOUS INSPIRATION must run in the family. When he was small, my son Ben liked to visit Mother and Tabb in Thomasville.

At breakfast once when he was five, Mother said, "Ben, I know you all have a box of Bible verses that you read at breakfast time. We don't have that, but will you say your favorite verse?"

In a deep voice, Ben responded, "You shalt not commit adultery."

Mother and Tabb—both then in their seventies—had to leave the table quickly.

MISS JULIA MARY Allen taught my first and second grade Sunday School class. She taught us the Bible alphabet. Each pupil was given a piece of heavy poster board with the sides of a ladder drawn on it. As scripture verses were memorized, they became steps on the ladder:

A - A soft answer turneth away wrath.

B - Be not hasty in thy spirit to be angry.

C - Christ Jesus came into the world to save sinners.

D - Do unto others as you would have them do unto you.

E - Even a child maketh himself known by his actions.

F - For God so loved the world that he gave His son.

G - God is love.

And so on.

She doubts it, but I can still recall nearly every step in our Bible ladders.

In our church the pipe from the big pot-bellied stove that heated our sanctuary ran along the ceiling from the front of the church, over the heads of the congregation, to a chimney in the rear.

One summer Sunday during the sermon, a wire holding the stove pipe broke, and one end of a section of pipe dropped and, like a funnel, poured years of accumulated soot right onto my playmate Tease.

Tease was the blondest child in Thomasville. She had naturally platinum hair, fair skin, and that day she was wearing a white dotted-Swiss dress that her grandmother had made for her.

In two seconds, she and her clothes were completely covered with black, black soot. It was a sight to behold!

Church, of course, broke up, and we all had to

be sent to the Baptists until the sanctuary could be cleaned up.

THAT WOULD NOT have been a first, however. On occasional summer Sunday nights Thomasville's Baptists and Methodists and others gathered in Clay Park. We sat on makeshift benches of concrete blocks and boards or in folding chairs and sang and prayed and listened to a short sermon. I'm sure that the collection was divided between the denominations, but I don't know how. *She*, remarkably, doesn't remember either.

HONEY, *She* SHRANK ME

Soon after *She* took up residence, I began to notice that I was shrinking. I was about two inches shorter than I used to be. I could no longer reach the top shelves in the linen closet or the higher shelves in the kitchen.

She laughed when I tried to get a box of oatmeal down from a shelf in the kitchen. "I tried to tell you that those shelves were too high, but you wouldn't listen," *She* said. I could not argue.

Unfortunately, the same problem existed with the lowest shelves of the pantry and closets. I could not bend low enough or stretch far enough to reach what I needed. Something had to be done.

The solution in the kitchen was easy. I simply stored canned goods and other non-perishable items in the oven. Living alone, I never use that oven except for family occasions and every January 1st when friends gather at my house to eat black-eyed peas and cornbread (with no sugar). Then I baked several pans of cornbread in that oven. The rest of the time I found that a counter-top toaster oven met all my baking needs.

She hooted at the oven storage solution, but it was practical solution, and so I paid no attention to her. At this moment, my oven holds a box of cereal, spaghetti, whole-grain breakfast bars, marshmallows, Triskets, two cans of diced tomatoes, a can of sliced peaches, and several other items. I could probably open a small grocery store right out of my oven.

NOT ONLY HAVE I shrunk in height since *She* came into my life, I have also shrunk in width and girth. Most of my favorite garments are too big.

When I complained about my change in size, blaming it all on her, *She* retorted, "You've got too many clothes anyway. You've got to give some to Goodwill and the Salvation Army."

She was right, of course. There are clothes in my

closets that I have not worn in ten years.

"But I'm a child of the Great Depression!" I explained. We did not throw anything away."

She was not impressed.

Once again I was pushed into a project I would neither enjoy nor finish. But I got a big box and prepared to fill it with garments for donation. I hate to make decisions, and every garment in my closet requested a decision. Besides, the seasons are changing, and I might gain weight. And there might be occasions when I need to wear a dress like this, I said, as I held one up for *She* to inspect. "Hah!" *She* replied.

The box is still empty. Indecision seems to be an affliction that worsens with age.

On the other hand, a box of kitchen utensils, coffee cups, plates, glasses, and such is filled and ready to go to the Salvation Army.

"Why would one woman need all this stuff in her kitchen?" *She* asked as we packed the box. "Why did you need three cast-iron skillets or three big pots or goodness knows how many glasses? And how many old-fashioned can openers did you have?"

To the can opener question, I reminded her that when I got married at the end of World War II, the usual wedding gifts were not available. A popular alternative gift was an electric can opener; I got seven of them. My doctor told me to give them all away and to open cans with the traditional kind that required hand and finger power instead of electricity.

"You will never have arthritis in your right hand if you do that," he promised.

I took his advice. Through the years, I accumulated quite an assortment of manually operated can openers as I tried to find a model that opened a can smoothly and efficiently. I never found it, but I did build up an impressive collection of the devices.

Only in the last year or two did I acquire an electric model, and I'm not exactly sure how it got into my kitchen although I do recognize it as a part of the electrification process I described earlier.

I remember standing in the kitchen and for the first time really paying attention to the electric can opener. "You are the first permanent electric appliance brought into this house in recent years," I accused it. "You must be in cahoots with *She*. You both sneaked up on me. Because you did not have a long cord, I did not recognize that you were a harbinger of things to come."

"You are slow to catch on," *She* said.

So it all started with an electric can opener. And it doesn't work very well, either.

DESPITE NAGGING ME about my surplus of possessions, *She* does not always contribute to improvement of the situation. One recent day with mild temperature, I suggested that we continue giving away and clearing out by tackling the accumulation of stuff in what was once my garage. For many years my car has sat outside in the weather because the garage had become the resting place for stuff not in use but too good to throw away or that might be needed later.

I unlocked the building with anticipation and good intentions, but *She* took one look and turned away.

"Looks like rain," *She* said. "If it rains, the humidity in there will be intolerable. We will try another day."

For all her cantankerousness, I have to admit that sometimes *She* and I are birds of a feather.

She AND PALLBEARERS

Years ago my sister Annelee used to call me from Thomasville every now and then and say, "Please come to see me and bring an indelible pencil. I need to change my pallbearers."

Annelee was not a patient woman and waiting did not wear well with her, so I would set out immediately on the sixty-five-mile drive, but without an indelible pencil. Daddy had some in the bank but I haven't seen one in years. I substituted a fine-point permanent marker and hoped it would meet her requirements.

I tried hard and usually unsuccessfully to please Annelee. I was born the night she graduated from high school and she never forgave me. "Nobody was the least bit interested in my graduation. Everybody was excited about the new baby," she used to complain.

When I was grown she told me that my birth

was a surprise to her: nobody told her about the expected baby. *She* finds that difficult to believe. Surely a senior in high school must have been aware that her mother was pregnant and must have wondered where she went and why she was away from home for more than a month.

When I arrived at her home after a pallbearer summons, Annelee would give me a brief greeting and then instruct me to look in the small drawer on the right-hand side of the chest of drawers in her bedroom for the small notebook she kept there. I was quite familiar with the notebook and its location. I assured her that I had brought a proper pencil to write with.

"Now read me the list of my pallbearers."

I did, and she was quiet for a few minutes. "Take Paul off," she said. "I hear he is getting old and feeble. I'll probably outlive him. And take Tom off. He has a beautiful voice, and I'd rather he sing in the choir."

She hesitated a minute or two. "Then there's Jeff. He has been on my list longer than anybody else, but it has been at least four months since he came to see me. Take him off! And Massey, I hear he was arrested for gambling when the sheriff raided the Silver Slipper last week. Be sure to take him off."

Then would come the problem of replacing the cast-offs. Each candidate for pallbearer had to be evaluated by health status, family or friend-ship connections, personal reputation, and spiritual worthiness. It was much easier to get off Annelee's pallbearer list than to get on it.

For years I laughed at what I called Annelee's "peculiar pastime." Now of course I find myself doing the same thing. It is amazing how time can change outlook.

IN THE UPPER right-hand drawer of my desk is a notebook with the names of my pallbearers written in it. Reading the list is depressing: So many of my prospective graveyard ushers have died. Some have moved far away. Some I cannot recall how they qualified for the list in the first place.

She laughs at me and teases me about following

my sister's example, the example I made fun of for years. But I find that choosing and reviewing pall-bearers is enjoyable, that it stirs many memories that make good stories. *She* does not entirely comprehend what constitutes good therapy and entertainment.

"Now there's Jim," I explain. "He has been on my pallbearer list longer than anybody else. Know why? He brings me rattlesnake rattles."

She does not understand and I'm not sure I do, either, but I do know that if I had an indelible pencil I would use it to write Jim's name.

AFTER SHE FINISHED fine-tuning her list of pall-bearers, Annelee would also go over with me the plans for her funeral, the hymns she wanted sung and the scripture she wanted read. Actually, it was the after-burial activities that concerned her most. "I don't want the church to provide the meal for the family and out-of-town guests, and I don't want folks bringing casseroles and fried chicken and cakes to the house. I want simpler finger food, sandwiches, and cookies served here."

Then she would remind me which platters and trays she wanted to be used and where each one was located in her house. All this was written in her neat handwriting in the back of the pallbearer notebook, but she wanted to be sure I was aware of her wishes.

Much to *She*'s amusement, my own funeral plans have been made, too. Who better to plan the event than the honoree? I want to be buried next to my husband and daughter at New Live Oak Cemetery within twenty-four hours after my death. A prompt burial will make it possible for me to avoid the funeral home entirely. I will not have to be embalmed, nor will I require a vault.

My grave, however, will have to be six feet deep and that may present a minor problem for somebody. Not me! Another small problem will be getting the Rose Point crystal service out of my coffin where it has been stored for more than twenty years.

I do not want a pall covering my coffin. I want everybody to admire the beauty of John Moss's craftsmanship.

Father Joe Knight of St. Paul's Episcopal Church will conduct the graveside service, using the Methodist ritual for the burial of the dead; and whoever is pastor of Church Street United Methodist Church will say a final short prayer.

Then Gordon Welch, minister of music at Church Street, will lead whoever attends the service in playing "I'll Fly Away" on combs. Gordon already has the bright blue combs and wax paper for use by the musicians.

I, like Annelee, want to decline a meal at the church or at my home. After the cemetery service, people who want to can come to my house and drink anything they can find. And maybe tell a few stories. I'd like that.

She considers it unbecoming to publish my funeral plans, but I feel relieved to have let friends and family know my wishes.

Editor's Postscript

Kathryn Tucker Windham's long and remarkably creative and productive life came to an end on Sunday, June 12, 2011, just ten days after she had celebrated her ninety-third birthday. She died quietly, surrounded by her loved ones, in the home on Selma's Royal Street where she had lived for decades.

In keeping with her burial wishes, she was laid to rest the next morning in a small, private graveside service. I later asked her son Ben Windham if the preparations and the funeral and the aftermath had gone more or less as she outlined in the last chapter of this, her last book.

"Everything was just so," Ben said.

A WEEK LATER, there was a public memorial service at Church Street United Methodist Church. Some five hundred people crowded in to pay their last respects. Her minister, the Reverend Fred Zeigler, officiated. Her friend and fellow storyteller/author Donald Davis gave the eulogy. The Dill Pickers string band performed several numbers and Norton Dill, director of the 2004 documentary, *Kathryn: The Story of a Teller*, gave a personal tribute. Gordon Welch played the organ and led the Chancel Choir Combs in a spirited rendition of "When We All Get to Heaven." The congregation joined in singing her favorite song, "I'll Fly Away."

> *Some glad morning when this life is o'er, I'll fly away;*
> *To a home on God's celestial shore, I'll fly away.*
>
> *I'll fly away, O Glory, I'll fly away;*
> *When I die, Hallelujah, by and by, I'll fly away.*

And she did.

KATHRYN CALLED ME with the idea for this book

sometime in the fall of 2010. NewSouth's publisher Suzanne La Rosa and I drove over to Selma and sat around the famous pine table—it had not yet been pushed against the wall—and she fed us vegetable soup and cornbread and we talked about the book. She had already filled a couple of legal pads with stories, and she read some aloud to us. We left bearing a sheaf of pages to type up and start the editing process.

Over the next several months, I visited a few more times and each time she presented more pages and we talked about the structure and the device she had come up with of an alter ego, *She*. In early 2011, Kathryn had a bad spell and was hospitalized, followed by a period of rehabilitation. By early spring, however, she was feeling better and was back at work.

By the time she was hospitalized and then in rehabilitation for the last time in late spring, the manuscript was reasonably complete and we were well into editing. Kathryn said she didn't know what to do about an ending, so we were still working on that. When she died before publication, the pallbearers chapter became the obvious ending. I continued to edit along the lines of our final conversations, and Ben offered his suggestions.

The result is what you have here. I believe she—and *She*—would be pleased.

— RANDALL WILLIAMS